The Story of Jesus

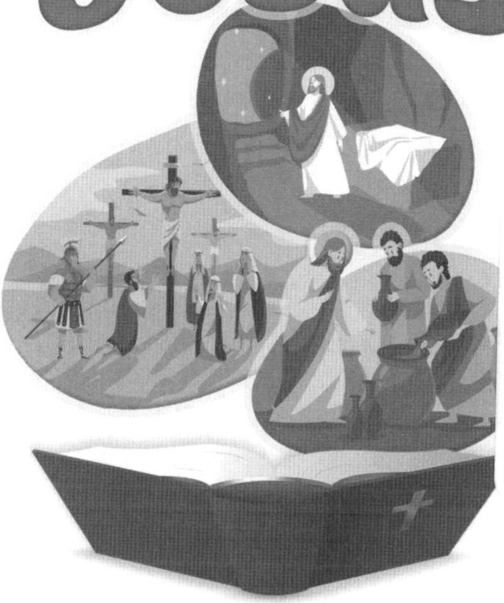

itty-bitty **Easter Activity Book**

E4903

3058002100000324

God loved us so much that He sent His Son, Jesus, to the world. Jesus came as a tiny baby. He was called the light of the world.

Circle 8 kinds of light hidden in the manger scene below.

(ANSWERS ON PAGE 46)

Every year Jesus' parents went to Jerusalem for the Feast of the Passover. When Jesus was 12, He got to go with them.

Help Jesus and His family reach Jerusalem.

(ANSWERS ON PAGE 46)

On the way home, Jesus' parents couldn't find Him. They went back to Jerusalem and found Jesus in the temple, talking to the teachers.

Connect the dots.

(ANSWERS ON PAGE 46)

The time came for Jesus to begin His work. He wanted to be baptized first. When He came up from the water, God sent down His Spirit in the form of a dove.

What did God say? Use the code to find out.

__ __ __   __ __ __   __ __
2 4 17   5 1 13   6 2

__ __ __,   __ __ __ __   __
7 4 9   8 10 4 6   11

__ __ __ __;   __ __ __ __
12 4 3 13   8 11 14 10

__ __ __   __   __ __   __ __ __ __
2 4 17   11   5 6   8 13 12 12

__ __ __ __ __ __ __.
15 12 13 5 7 13 16

Luke 3:22 (NIV)

(ANSWERS ON PAGE 46)

Jesus chose 12 men called disciples to help with His work. Which men did Jesus choose?

(ANSWERS ON PAGE 46)

Solve the math problems.
If the answer is 12, color the disciple.

$5 \times 3 =$ ____

$24 \div 2 =$ ____

$15 - 3 =$ ____

$9 + 7 =$ ____

$15 - 7 =$ ____

$7 + 5 =$ ____

$2 + 10 =$ ____

$12 \times 1 =$ ____

(ANSWERS ON PAGE 46)

Jesus did many different things as part of His work. Some of them are listed below.

Circle the words in the puzzle.

K	W	N	E	B	F	X	J	S	L	N	T	Y	M
T	O	R	Q	Z	I	O	Z	U	O	P	B	I	Y
O	R	A	U	A	E	Q	R	G	K	R	R	N	G
O	S	A	E	N	T	Z	D	O	X	A	S	A	M
I	H	C	V	Q	E	Z	Z	T	C	Y	Z	Q	F
S	I	J	U	E	I	E	G	L	D	Y	K	Z	B
B	P	N	F	G	L	N	E	W	I	C	Q	W	D
Y	O	I	W	K	K	S	Q	Q	S	K	N	P	Y
K	J	J	K	U	G	E	X	H	Q	Q	H	E	Q
D	G	N	Q	L	V	R	O	C	D	J	G	T	Z
P	Y	X	K	S	R	C	K	L	M	H	H	K	B
I	Q	T	F	T	B	T	D	H	Z	L	A	E	Q
K	I	G	J	S	K	L	C	T	I	L	A	G	J
V	E	N	J	Q	C	A	I	Y	M	E	T	E	X
S	A	I	S	P	E	E	S	Z	B	X	D	A	H
O	L	S	D	T	Y	D	F	R	W	Z	G	H	E

HEAL	PRAY	TRAVEL	EAT
MIRACLES	TEACH	SING	WORSHIP

(ANSWERS ON PAGE 46)

People came from miles around to ask Jesus to heal them or their loved ones. Jesus healed many who were sick or hurt.

Use the list of conditions Jesus healed to fill in the grid.

BLIND DEAF LEPROSY LAME CRIPPLED
BLEEDING FEVER MUTE PARALYZED DEAD

(ANSWERS ON PAGE 46)

Jesus and His disciples headed toward Jerusalem for the Passover celebration. Jesus told them to bring an animal for Him to ride.

Connect the dots.

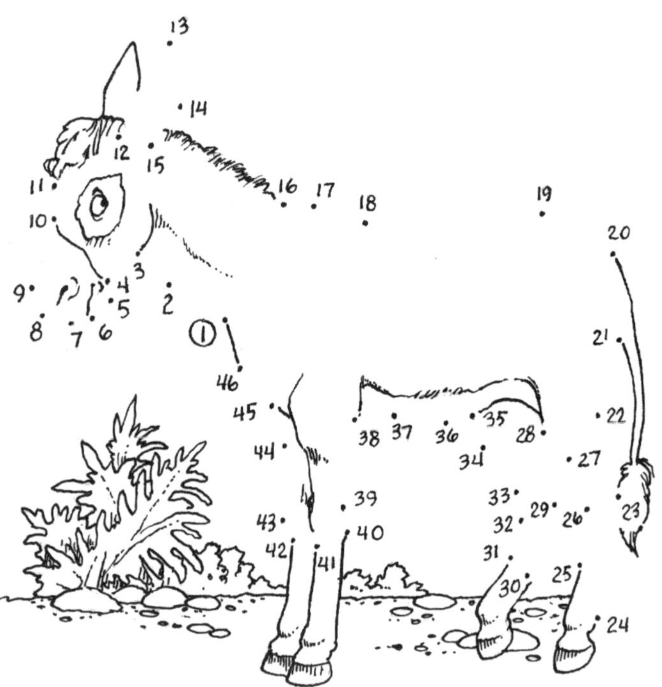

(ANSWERS ON PAGE 46)

A crowd was waiting for Jesus.
They were so excited to see Him!

Circle the hidden palm branches.

How many do you see? ____

(ANSWERS ON PAGE 46)

The people had heard about the miracles and other wonderful things Jesus had done.

Circle the hidden pictures: cross, coin, crown, mug, glass of water, arrow, anchor, and apple.

(ANSWERS ON PAGE 46)

The people shouted and waved to welcome Jesus.

Write the first letter of each picture to see what the people were waving.

(ANSWERS ON PAGE 46)

Many people who welcomed Jesus threw their robes on the ground for Jesus' donkey to walk on.

Find the underlined words in the puzzle below and color them in. Then write the letters you did not color on the lines to find out what the people shouted to welcome Jesus.

____ ____ ____ ____ ____ ____ ____!

Matthew 21:9 (NIV)

(ANSWERS ON PAGE 46)

Jesus' many followers were loudly praising God. Some men who didn't like Jesus told Him to make the people be quiet. Jesus said that if the people stopped praising Him, the stones would cry out.

Draw faces on the stones, so they can shout praise to God!

People in the city asked, "Who is this?" What did the crowds answer?

Color in the spaces with dots to find out.

"This is ___ ___ ___ ___ ___." Matthew 21:11 (NIV)

(ANSWERS ON PAGE 46)

A woman poured expensive perfume on Jesus' head from an alabaster jar. Some of the disciples thought she was wasting money. Jesus defended her. He said, "She did this to prepare me for burial."

Color the spaces with dots.

(ANSWERS ON PAGE 47)

One day Judas, one of the disciples, went to the powerful rulers who hated Jesus and offered to show them where Jesus was.

The men said they would pay Judas.

How much was Judas paid? Write the letter that comes BEFORE the letter under the line.

(ANSWERS ON PAGE 47)

Jesus ate one last Passover meal with His disciples.

Circle the hidden pictures: fish, cross, Bible, cat, dog, saw, arrow, and anchor.

(ANSWERS ON PAGE 47)

What is another name for that special meal?

Follow the dotted lines to each cross.
Then write the cross' letter in the box.

(ANSWERS ON PAGE 47)

Jesus shared bread and wine with the disciples.
He said this was a symbol of His body and blood.
What do we call it when we share the
bread and juice at church?

Complete the dot-to-dot. Then find and circle 9 hidden letters. Put them in the correct order to read the word.

____ ____ ____ ____ ____ ____ ____ ____ ____

(ANSWERS ON PAGE 47)

After the meal, Jesus took Peter, James, and John with Him to the Mount of Olives.

What did Jesus want to do there?
Color the spaces with dots to find out.

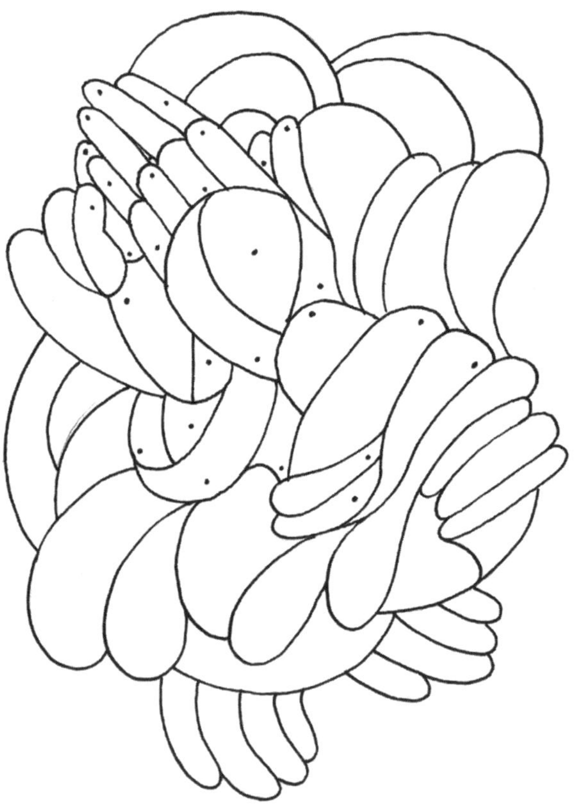

(ANSWERS ON PAGE 47)

Jesus said all the disciples would leave Him. Peter said he would never do that. Jesus said Peter would deny Him three times before a certain animal made a noise.

What was the animal?
Color in the spaces with dots to find out.

(ANSWERS ON PAGE 47)

In the garden, Jesus prayed that "this cup" would pass from Him. He was talking about a "cup of suffering"—or His death. But Jesus promised He would obey God's will, no matter what.

Find the two cups that are exactly alike.

(ANSWERS ON PAGE 47)

While Jesus prayed, the disciples were so tired they kept falling asleep.

Help Jesus find the way back to His disciples.

(ANSWERS ON PAGE 47)

Just as Jesus finished praying, Judas brought soldiers to capture Him. They arrested Jesus, even though He had done nothing wrong.

Find the path from Jesus and Judas to the soldiers.

(ANSWERS ON PAGE 47)

Soldiers arrested Jesus.
They took Him away to the courts.

Circle the hidden pictures: heart, Bible, crown, cup, umbrella, belt, candle, arrow, and bottle.

(ANSWERS ON PAGE 47)

After Jesus' arrest, all His disciples ran away—including Peter. People asked Peter, "Aren't you one of Jesus' followers?" Three times Peter said no. Then he heard the rooster crow, just as Jesus said he would.

What did Peter do when he realized he had broken his promise to Jesus?

Write the first letter of each picture to find out.

From Matthew 26:75 (NIV)

(ANSWERS ON PAGE 47)

Soldiers took Jesus to a judge named Pilate. The judge knew Jesus was not guilty. He asked the people, "What should I do with Jesus?" What did the people shout?

Cross out every G, P, and Z. Then write the letters you have left on the lines to read the answer.

_ _ _ _ _ _ _   _ _ _!

Matthew 27:22 (NIV)

(ANSWERS ON PAGE 47)

Since the Jewish people had been calling Jesus a king, soldiers decided to treat Him like a pretend king. They took His own clothes away. Then they gave Jesus a purple robe, the color kings wore.

Color the picture using the code below.

1=RED 2=BLUE 3=ORANGE 4=GREEN 5=YELLOW

The soldiers made fun of Jesus and hit Him. They put something on His head. What was it?

Color the spaces with dots to find out.

(ANSWERS ON PAGE 47)

Roman soldiers placed a heavy cross on Jesus' back. They made Him walk a long way through the winding streets of Jerusalem to a place called Golgotha, which means "the place of the Skull."

Find the path from Jesus to Golgotha.

(ANSWERS ON PAGE 48)

Jesus was already hurting so much from His cuts and bruises that He could hardly stand. The soldiers nailed Jesus to the cross.

Find and circle the letters J E S U S in the picture.

(ANSWERS ON PAGE 48)

The soldiers cast lots to see who would get Jesus' clothes. They didn't know they were fulfilling a prophecy in the Bible about Jesus.

Write the underlined words in the boxes where they fit.

They divide my clothes among them
and cast lots for my garment.

Psalm 22:18 (NIV)

(ANSWERS ON PAGE 48)

Two robbers were on crosses beside Jesus. One thief realized who Jesus was and asked Jesus to remember him. Jesus promised the thief a place in heaven because he believed.

What did Jesus do to the thief? Follow the lines from the letters to the boxes. Then write the letters to read the word.

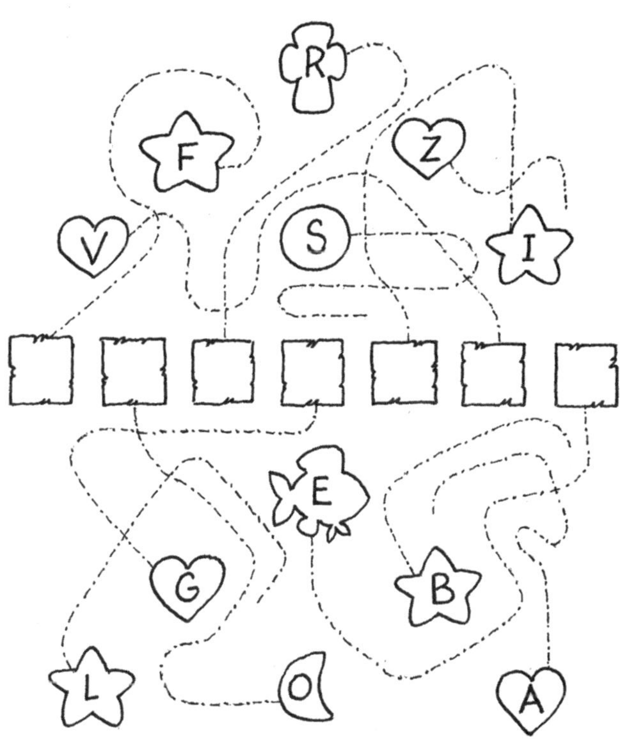

(ANSWERS ON PAGE 48)

When Jesus died, darkness covered the earth, even though it was still daytime. There was a loud earthquake, and rocks split in two. People were very afraid.

Find and circle the words in the puzzle.

AFRAID	DARKNESS	FEAR	SAFE
CALM	DAYLIGHT	JESUS	STORM
CANDLE	EARTHQUAKE	LIGHT	WORLD

```
W N M N X I M X F U J L
E O V V Z P Z Y O E I F
M A R C W S U J S G E U
E H R L A U C U H A R D
T W I T D L S T R N A D
H N D N H T M P N R I L
G D R M B Q M D K W I P
I W I C M P U N O O J S
L M A A T R E A K E A J
Y M K K R S O X K F W Y
A Q I B S F Z T E E P Y
D R E L D N A C S V V U
```


(ANSWERS ON PAGE 48)

The curtain of the temple was torn from top to bottom. That curtain hid the special place where only the priests could go. With the torn curtain, God was saying to us, "Because Jesus died for your sins, you can come into God's presence yourself."

What did the centurion guarding Jesus say?
Use the code to find out.

14 17 13 15 4 23

24 15   20 3 14   16 24 15

14 8 7   8 18   21 8 12 !

Matthew 27:54 (NIV)

(ANSWERS ON PAGE 48)

After Jesus died, a kind man wrapped Jesus' body in a linen cloth and laid it in a new tomb. A huge stone was rolled in front of the door, and soldiers guarded it.

Circle the hidden pictures: mug, perfume bottle, cross, turtle, lily, grapes, dove, Bible

(ANSWERS ON PAGE 48)

When Jesus' friends came to the tomb three days later, the stone was rolled away! An angel spoke to them.

What did the angel say? Use the code to find out.

13	14	15	16	17	18	19	20	21	22	23	24	25
A	**B**	**C**	**D**	**E**	**F**	**G**	**H**	**I**	**J**	**K**	**L**	**M**
26	1	2	3	4	5	6	7	8	9	10	11	12
N	**O**	**P**	**Q**	**R**	**S**	**T**	**U**	**V**	**W**	**X**	**Y**	**Z**

___ ___ ___ ___ ___ ___ ___ ___ ___
21 23 26 1 9 6 20 13 6

___ ___ ___ ___ ___ ___
11 1 7 13 4 17

___ ___ ___ ___ ___ ___ ___
24 1 1 23 21 26 19

___ ___ ___ ___ ___ ___ ___ ___....
18 1 4 22 17 5 7 5

___ ___ ___ ___ ___ ___ ___
20 17 21 5 26 1 6

___ ___ ___ ___; ___ ___
20 17 4 17 20 17

___ ___ ___ ___ ___ ___ ___ ___.
20 13 5 4 21 5 17 26

Matthew 28:5–6 (NIV)

(ANSWERS ON PAGE 48)

Mary Magdalene had been crying. When she heard Jesus speak her name, she knew He really was alive again. She was so excited she told the disciples that Jesus was alive.

Find and circle the words in the puzzle.

WOMEN	STONE	JESUS	HE
TOMB	ROLLED	ANGEL	RISEN

Q S Z Y S T O N L G E

U T E A P A N G E L W

R O I T R I S E N S O

O M F W O B E N A T M

L B J O H Q M A F O E

L E A M O U R J A N S

E A S E V R O L L E D

R M U N H I V I C L X

S A S J E S U S H F O

(ANSWERS ON PAGE 48)

Later, the disciples were gathered in a room with the doors locked. Just then, a man appeared in the room. "Peace be with you," He said. Who was this man?

Color the spaces with dots to find out.

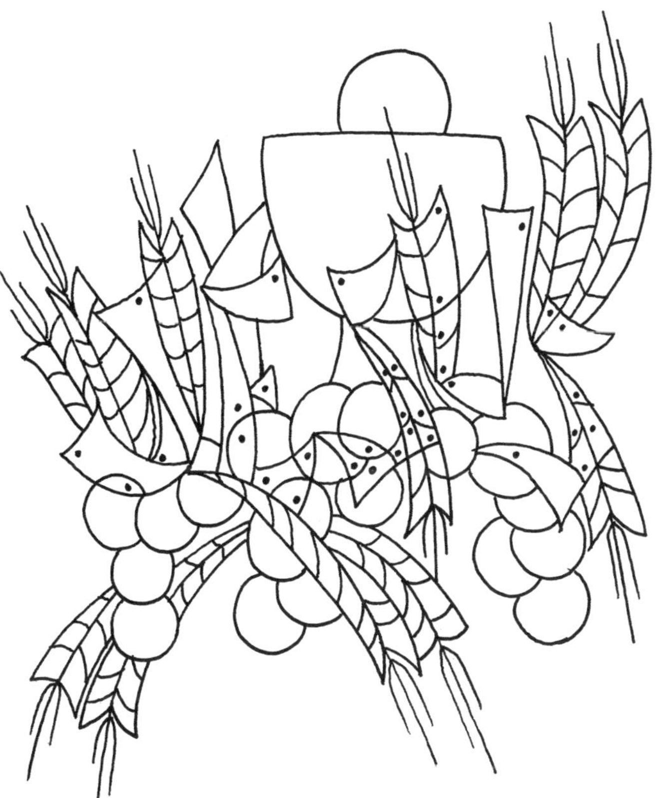

(ANSWERS ON PAGE 48)

Jesus reminded the disciples of what the Bible says. He helped them understand the meaning of the Scriptures. What had Jesus told the disciples?

Start at the arrow and cross out every Z. Then fill in the blanks with the letters you DID NOT cross out.

AZYSZ⇨IZZWZ
Z Z
D I
ZREZZZE LZLZLZC
Z O
Z Z
H M
Z Z
Z E
TZNZ ZAZZ
I C Z
Z Z B
Z K
Z Z
E Z
Z T
Z
ZFZZIZZLZOZ

From Luke 24:46

“ ___ ___ ___ ___ ___ ___ ___ ___ ___

___ ___ ___ ___ ___ ___ ___ ___ ___ ___ ___

___ ___ ___ ___ ___ ___ ___ ___ ___ ___ ___ ___ ___.”

(ANSWERS ON PAGE 48)

Jesus began to bless His disciples. Then they watched as Jesus rose in the clouds to go back to heaven. The disciples were filled with joy. They worshiped Jesus and began telling others about Him.

Connect the dots.

(ANSWERS ON PAGE 48)

It's sad to think of how much Jesus hurt. We may wonder why someone didn't stop it. But God loved us so much, He gave His only Son, Jesus, to die for us so we could be a part of God's family.

Circle the hidden pictures: Bible, crown, dove, lily, cross, sword, cup, heart

(ANSWERS ON PAGE 48)

Because Jesus died and rose again, we can have a great gift when we ask Him into our hearts!

What is the gift? Color the spaces with dots to find out.

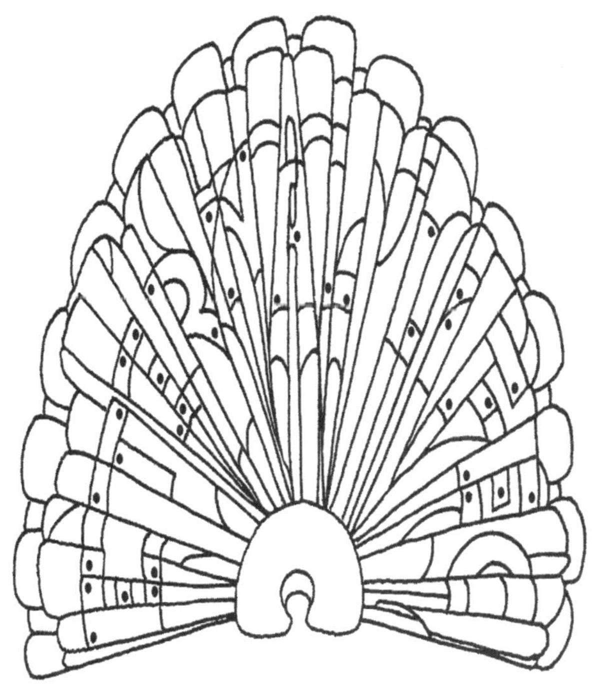

(ANSWERS ON PAGE 48)

PAGE 2

PAGE 3

PAGE 4

PAGE 5

You are my Son, whom I love; with you I am well pleased.

PAGE 6-7

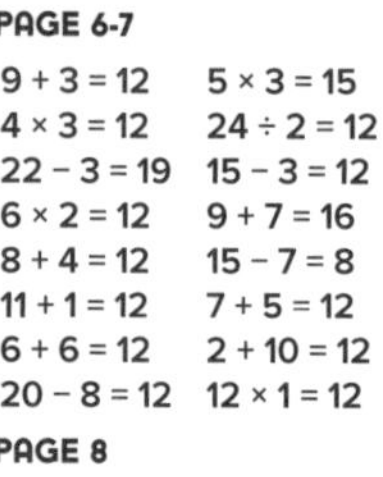

9 + 3 = 12	5 × 3 = 15
4 × 3 = 12	24 ÷ 2 = 12
22 − 3 = 19	15 − 3 = 12
6 × 2 = 12	9 + 7 = 16
8 + 4 = 12	15 − 7 = 8
11 + 1 = 12	7 + 5 = 12
6 + 6 = 12	2 + 10 = 12
20 − 8 = 12	12 × 1 = 12

PAGE 8

K W N E B F X J S L N T Y M
T O R Q Z I O Z U O P B I Y
O R A U A E Q R G K R R N G
O S A E N T Z D O X A S A M
I H C V Q E Z Z T C Y Z Q F
S I J U E I E G L D Y K Z B
B P N F G L N E W I C Q W D
Y O I W K K S Q Q S K N P Y
K J J K U G E X H Q Q H E Q
D G N Q L V R O C D J G T Z
P Y X K S R C K L M H H K B
I Q T F T B T D H Z L A E Q
K I G J S K L C T I L A G J
V E N J Q C A I Y M E T E X
S A I S P E E S Z B X D A H
O L S D T Y D F R W Z G H E

PAGE 9

PAGE 10

PAGE 11 7 branches

PAGE 12

PAGE 13

PALM BRANCHES

PAGE 14

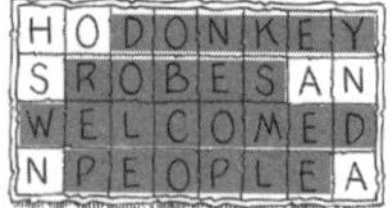

H	O	D	O	N	K	E	Y
S	R	O	B	E	S	A	N
W	E	L	C	O	M	E	D
N	P	E	O	P	L	E	A

HOSANNA

PAGE 16

PAGE 17

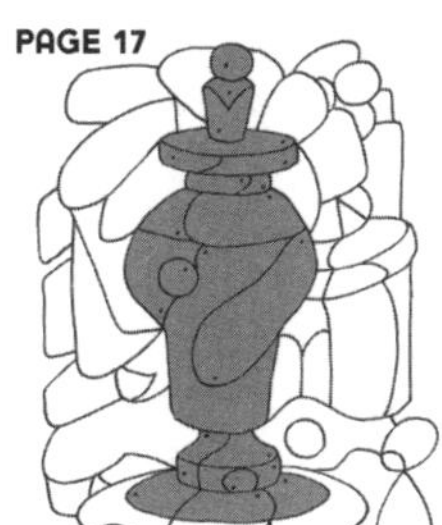

PAGE 18

THIRTY SILVER COINS

PAGE 19

PAGE 20

LAST SUPPER

PAGE 21

COMMUNION

PAGE 22

PAGE 23

PAGE 24

PAGE 25

PAGE 26

START

PAGE 27

PAGE 28

PETER WEPT BITTERLY

PAGE 29

CRUCIFY HIM!

PAGE 31

ANSWERS

PAGE 32

PAGE 33

JESUS

PAGE 34

						C			
				T		L	O	T	S
				H		O			
G	A	R	M	E	N	T			
	M			M		H			
	O					E			
	N			C	A	S	T		
	G						H		
		D	I	V	I	D	E		
							M		

PAGE 35

FORGIVE

PAGE 36

PAGE 37

SURELY HE WAS THE SON OF GOD!

PAGE 38

PAGE 39

I KNOW THAT YOU ARE LOOKING FOR JESUS...HE IS NOT HERE; HE HAS RISEN.

PAGE 40

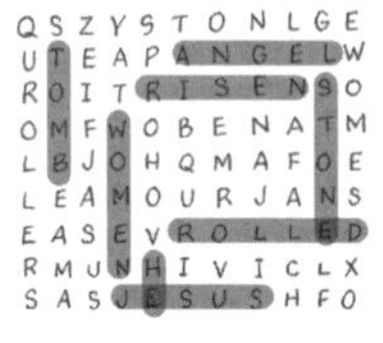

PAGE 41

PAGE 42

I WILL COME BACK TO LIFE IN THREE DAYS.

PAGE 43

PAGE 44

PAGE 45